OZZIE'S ODYSSEY

*My life before and after
the MV Christena went down*

By Oswald Tyson

Published by the Author under the auspices of the Nevis Historical and Conservation Society

Copyright © 2011 by Oswald Tyson

All rights reserved. No part of this book may be reproduced or transmitted in any form by any means, electronic or mechanical, including photocopying, recording, or by any information storage or retrieval system--except by a reviewer who may quote brief passages in a review to be printed in a magazine or newspaper--without permission in writing from the author.

ACKNOWLEDGEMENTS

I thank Evelyn Henville, Executive Director of the Nevis Historical and Conservation Society, for her support.

Thanks to Amba Trott and Vince Hubbard for their kind remarks.

Thanks to Dianne Collins, Paula Flemming and Amba Trott for their editorial comments.

Thanks to Donald and Paula Flemming for their encouragement to begin and to complete this undertaking.

Ozzie Tyson
Cotton Ground, Nevis
January 2011

DEDICATED TO:

Theodora Tyson

Rosamond Parris

Florence "Queen" Jones

Geoffrey and Sarah Sorenson

Donald and Paula Flemming

FOREWORD

This little volume of personal narrative is a welcome addition to our collection of oral history. Ozzie's story is the story of many Nevisians, and his memories of the past fifty years will help us all to recall the odyssey of our beloved Island.

Evelyn Henville
Executive Director
Nevis Historical and Conservation Society

EDITORS' NOTE

This is the story of Ozzie Tyson. Our function has been to get Ozzie to tell his story and then to transcribe what he has narrated into the text, which follows. The following quote from *One Thousand Roads to Mecca* by Michael Wolfe best expresses what we have attempted to do.

I have rendered the sense of the narrative in language that adequately expresses the purposes he had in mind, and I have set forth clearly the ends he had in view. Frequently I have reported his words in his own phrasing without omitting either root or branch.

Though the reader may not hear Ozzie's voice in the following pages, we invite you to listen to the singing and the crying of his soul.

Donald and Paula Flemming

PROLOGUE

A tiny island in the Eastern Caribbean rises from the sea with its long dormant volcano figuring prominently in its center. Some ten thousand souls of African descent inhabit this once unspoiled land of sun and sea. These children of the Diaspora have survived the Middle Passage and three centuries of harsh slavery as they worked the cane fields and cared for the master's every need.

They have survived more than a hundred additional years of colonial rule during which they were free only to be poor. They have survived earthquakes and hurricanes and man-made disasters, the most important of which was the sinking of the ferry boat, the *MV Christena*. This is the story of a survivor, a story unique in its detail and universal in its demonstration of the resilience of the human spirit.

This is the story of Oswald Tyson.

Listen, Dear Reader! I'm going to tell you a story. It's a long story, but not too long. It's got some funny parts, but it's got some sad parts too. This is a story about how I learned what I learned. This is what I want you to know. So listen, everyone! I want you all to hear my story.

CHAPTER I

You see, Mommy Dear--that's what I called my Mom--was living up in Cotton Ground in a high house owned by a lady name of Gwendolyn Atherton. Yes, she was the great-grandma of the fella who's now Premier of Nevis, Mr. Joseph Parry! Well, anyway, Mommy Dear got mixed up with this guy from Fountain, Frederick Liburd, and, in all due time, she was ready to birth me. So she called in Mrs. Chapman, the local midwife, and into this world came Oswald Tyson. You know, it was some time before I learned when that happened. Turns out it was April 17, 1959. Man, that sure was a long time ago! You know I'm a big guy today. Well, I was always big. When I was born, I weighed twelve pounds and fourteen ounces. Imagine that!

Seems like my father didn't want any part of me cause after Mommy Dear took him to court for child support, he took off for England. He's never been back. Not once. I did see a picture of him one time. His mother showed it to me. I was not sad or angry, just curious. Turns out I look just like him--at least that's what lots of folks have told me.

Well, Mommy Dear wanted to get me baptized, so she asked the Methodist minister to do it. She asked him 'cause that was the church she went to. Well, that fella wasn't very Christian in my estimation. He said because Mommy Dear had never married, I was a bastard, and he wouldn't baptize me. Well, Mommy Dear wouldn't give up. No, not her.

So she went and asked the Catholic priest whose name was Father Roberge. He had come down from Canada to start up a parish. Well, it seems like he was more in tune with what Jesus had to say about little children. He told Mommy Dear, "Sure, I'll baptize him and bring him into the family of God." He was the first guy to save me but definitely not the last. However, when I was old enough to understand this story, I knew there was a lesson in it for me.

Mommy Dear asked two local ladies, Eunice and Augusta William of Cotton Ground, to serve as Godmothers. For Godfathers, she recruited Alfred Deshatlo and Extension Officer, Evan Nisbett, a man of considerable influence at that time whose son, Julian, now runs that convenience store across from the Newcastle airport.

Mommy Dear--I guess I should mention her name was Theodora Tyson--was a very talented seamstress. Everyone knew how skilled she was, so they brought clothes for repair and orders for new apparel as well. Mommy Dear sat at her pedal-operated Singer sewing machine most of the day and some of the night doing her best to serve her customers' needs.

But life was not easy for Mommy Dear. When I was born, she already had three older boys: Clyde, Patrick and Alex. Then, when I was about six months old, I got sick, and Mommy Dear had to take me to the hospital. She was sure the jumbies had got me and that I was going to die.

I never did find out exactly what was wrong with me, but I do know that the jumbies have troubled other folks on Nevis. Anyway, while I was in the hospital, the nurses began calling me Ozzie. You know, that name has stuck with me to this day. I'm sort of glad because I hate nicknames, so Ozzie is better than other things they might have called me!

CHAPTER II

When I was around three years old, Mommy Dear took me down to live with my great-aunt Rosamond Parris who was already in her nineties having been born in 1870. Mommy Dear thought Aunt Rose needed some company, and she decided I'd be the one. Aunt Rose had three chattel houses on the rise overlooking Nelson Springs.

Her sister, Frances Brazier, lived in one and my great-aunt, Lillian Dowell, in another. Aunt Rose and I lived in the one near the Island Road next to her garden. Even though she was a very old lady, she got out to the garden most every day weeding and watering and harvesting and, in general, keeping everything green and growing.

Aunt Rose's house was always spic and span. The floor was so clean you could have eaten off of it. Aunt Rose always told me, "Ozzie, cleanliness is next to godliness." And she practiced what she preached.

Aunt Rose was well educated and very religious. She taught Sunday School classes for adults in the local church. She insisted that I mind my manners and that I always act respectfully. If I didn't live up to her expectations, out came the broom, and I'd get a good beating. She was even strict with Mommy Dear, her grandniece! When she found out that Mommy Dear was pregnant again-- she never did marry, by the way--Aunt Rose picked up a stone and threw it at her. But Mommy Dear didn't turn the other cheek. She grabbed a bucket of water and threw it all over Aunt Rose.

In spite of her strictness, my happiest childhood memories are of sitting by Aunt Rose's side and listening to her stories about the history of Mommy Dear's family. She told me how the Europeans had brought Africans over to the Americas to work as slaves on the white man's plantations. She said many of the sailors who brought slaves from Africa were Portuguese because sailors from Portugal had long been exploring the West African coast while searching for a trade route to India. It seems that one of these Portuguese sailors took a fancy for a young African girl, and, as a result, my great-great-grandmother, Eunice Brown, was born.

Eunice was luckier than most slaves. First, since she was lighter-skinned than the other slaves, she was given a post of responsibility as caretaker of all the sheep on the plantation. Secondly, slavery came to an end in the British Caribbean when she was still young enough to enjoy many years of freedom. And she did have many years as a free woman for she lived to be 110 years old which gave Aunt Rose a chance to get to know her real well.

I wish I could have met her, but I feel I know her a little bit thanks to my dear Aunt Rose. Aunt Rose's sister, Eliza, was my great-grandmother. She married a man named Jeffords, and one of their daughters was my Grandmother Josephine. She married George Tyson, and one of their daughters, Theodora, is my Mommy Dear. So now you know a little about my roots.

CHAPTER III

One of my great-aunts was named Lillian Dowell. We called her "Red Ants" because she had reddish hair. She was a heavy woman, and, as a result, she walked very slowly.

She had a coal pot at her front door where she used to cook her favorite dish: steamed fish and dumplings which she made with cassava meal and coconut mixed up with flour. She would put the fish and dumplings on the coal pot to roast them. Then she would eat them and make soursop bush tea to drink. Whatever she had left over, she would save for the next day.

Great-aunt Lillian spent many years in the United States, from 1912 until 1952. While there, she experienced many hard times. However, she told us that she never was cold in the US. Her bed was always warm. One day, she went to see a shrink who told her that the reason she was never cold was because the feet of her grandmother, Eunice Brown, kept her warm. The shrink said that Eunice had followed Aunt Lillian from Nevis to New York. So Lillian came to believe that her dead grandmother had kept her bed warm for forty years!

Aunt Lillian also told us that her trip to the US was quite rough. Many people got seasick on the trip. In those days (1912), it took over five weeks to sail a schooner to the US. That is why many people who had gone to the US from Nevis never came back. They didn't want to face the sea journey again.

While in the States, Aunt Lillian sent for her youngest sister, Alberta France. Alberta settled in upstate New York and lived there until she died in 1987 at the age of 95. Aunt Alberta married in the US and had five children. Three of them were boys who all served in the military during World War II and the Korean War as well.

Aunt Lillian's husband raised sugar cane, but one of his neighbors kept stealing it. So Mr. Dowell told the thief that if he didn't stop, he would kill him. Well, the thief didn't stop, so Mr. Dowell confronted him in the cane field and killed him with a rock. He was taken into custody, charged with murder and hanged.

After Great-aunt Lillian returned to Nevis from the US, she always wore heavy socks! She had one daughter, Dora, before she went to the States. She left Nevis when Dora was only a few weeks old. So Lillian's mother, Eliza Parris, had to care for the little girl. Years later, Dora moved to Aruba and then to the US Virgin Islands where she died in 1996 at the age of 83.

Great-aunt Frances Brazier lost her sight, so Aunt Rose would go up to take care of her with me in tow. Aunt Frances's husband, Daniel, was a Methodist preacher. He was a large man, and while we were caring for Aunt Frances, he took sick. With eyes wide open, I watched him take quick short breaths like he was panting, and then I watched him die.

He was the first dead person I had ever seen. For some time after that, I had nightmares in which Brazier's ghost would appear in the room where I was sleeping. I sure am glad he didn't follow me for very long!

My brothers all stayed with Mommy Dear, except for Clyde who was much older and had already gone out on his own. I used to play with them from time to time. We would make cars and trucks out of the wood from sandbox trees. Dave was very smart, what people call a bookworm. I always thought he'd grow up to be somebody important. Dave loved to stay at home with Mommy Dear, and I'm sure he was her favorite. Even when he was very young, he made his own trucks to play with. He was always an obedient child. Kirsten was smart too.

Kirsten was my favorite because he always liked to help me. If I was cutting wood, he would help me carry the cut lengths. If I went to see our aunts in Barnes Ghaut or Jessups, he would come along. And if Mommy Dear told him he couldn't go, he would cry because he knew that whatever my aunts gave me, he would get his share. And if I was not at home when someone gave Kirsten some candy, he would save some for me. He started doing this when he was only two years old!

Growing up in Cotton Ground village was very rough. As far as I remember, only two families had cars: the Clarks and Wilmot Jones who had been a taxi driver since 1950. He still drives a taxi today, sixty years later, the oldest member of the Nevis fleet!

Nearly everyone cooked on a wood stove outdoors. Most people had a storeroom in the cellar which they used to keep the firewood dry and protected from the rain, which, of course, is essential if you want to cook with it.

Now, with few exceptions, the people in my village have gas or electric stoves as well as running water. When I was a boy, most people on Nevis had to carry water on their heads in buckets. Sometimes, when the weather was dry, they would come from miles around to draw water from Nelson's Spring.

Nelson's Spring is a National Historic Site as it was dug by Admiral Lord Nelson in 1787. It has produced water ever since. Admiral Nelson dug the well to provide water for his ships. The sailors would bring the barrels to the beach, roll them up to the well and fill them with water, a bucketful at a time, and then roll them back down to the beach. At that point they would take them back to the ships in preparation for the long sail back to England.

Luckily for me, the well is still flowing after 223 years. Now, I use the water to irrigate my fruit and vegetable plantings, but I no longer have to draw the water up in a bucket since I have installed an electric pump.

CHAPTER IV

Mommy Dear was having a hard time making ends meet, so she decided to go to Basseterre in St. Kitts to see if her work as a seamstress might pick up. She took me along with my brothers, Alex, Patrick, Dave and Kirsten, to live in the big city. Patrick and Alex were going to school, and since I was by now of school age, I cried to go with them. So Mommy Dear enrolled me in the Catholic school in town.

I soon learned that the nuns would not tolerate any nonsense or misbehavior. The sharp raps to the knuckles discouraged all but the most foolhardy miscreants. Luckily for me, they didn't subject me to rule by the ruler. In fact, I liked my teacher quite a bit.

Mommy Dear's hopes of a better life on St. Kitts failed to materialize, so she decided to go to St. Croix where she had relatives. I was sent back to live with Aunt Rose, and my brothers were placed with other relatives. My eldest brother Clyde was, by this time, living in Antigua. Those of us who remained on Nevis were sent to take meals at the home of Uncle Charles Tyson's girlfriend.

I was enrolled in St. Thomas School where I began to take an interest in history and geography. On weekdays, I would make sugar cakes and sell them at school during recess. My cakes sold out every day. Other children did the same thing, but my sugar cakes always seemed to be the most popular. Queen Jones, or Queenie as many called her, was the one who taught me how to make them.

I still remember too. You boil water with a lot of sugar in it. You add cinnamon bush and rose water for flavoring. When you have a thick syrup, you add shredded coconut to make a thick paste. Then you drop spoonfuls of the paste on a board or tray and let cool. That's all there is to it.

There were no school buses in those days. We had to walk back and forth to school. Every Tuesday, we would get a glass of milk at school provided by funds from the United Nations agency, UNICEF. Every Wednesday, we had to go to church for an hour at the St. Thomas Church School. We had to have all of our homework done before we arrived at school. If we arrived late, we got a whipping.

In 1966, the Queen of England and her husband paid a visit to Nevis that was still a colony of the United Kingdom. All the school children dressed in their uniforms. We had to go to Charlestown to greet Her Majesty and Prince Phillip. The couple arrived from St. Kitts on the royal yacht, Britannia. They took a smaller boat to the Charlestown pier.

The Chief Minister, Robert L. Bradshaw, ordered his men to roll out the red carpet on the pier for the Royal Family. As the Queen and her party came off the pier, the Police Band played "God Save Our Gracious Queen", Then we, the school children, sang "God Save the Queen". I can still remember this event as if it had taken place yesterday. The Queen was wearing a bright yellow dress. Prince Phillip was wearing a dark suit.

As the Queen walked off the pier, everyone, including me, shouted, "God save the Queen!" She started to wave to the crowd. Everyone, including Aunt Rose, was there. This was the largest crowd of people I have ever seen in one place on Nevis. There were babies and people over 100 years of age. The Queen departed in the Governor's car that carried the Royal couple to Government House and then to Fig Tree Church.

In 1966, Aunt Rose had a stroke, so Mommy Dear came home from St. Croix to care for her. Auntie held on for two months, but one day, an ambulance, a green Volkswagen bus, came for her and took her to the hospital. I knew I would never see her again. Her 96 years had come to an end. I loved Aunt Rose the most, and she loved me as well.

The chattel house on Aunt Rose's property where Mommy Dear set up home for me and my brothers had two rooms. We had no electricity, no running water, and we cooked on a wood-fired stove. Nevertheless, I was happy to be back with my family.

Dave and Kirsten joined me in attending St. Thomas School. Since I was the oldest, it was my job to look after them. Every day when his classes were over, Kirsten would appear at my classroom door waiting for me to take him home. Sometimes, when I rode my donkey to school, I would let Kirsten ride on the way home. He liked that a lot. In the little free time I had, I would play cricket on the sports field up behind St. Thomas School.

The teachers would supervise the games and make sure that we not only played by the rules but that we behaved in general. If we didn't, either they or the Principal would give us a beating. We'd get another one when we got home as someone would always run ahead to tattle on us.

I can't remember who my first girlfriend was, but I do recall that when we played hide-and-seek with the girls, we would take advantage of being out of view to, let me say, get to know each other more closely!

Mommy Dear, in addition to being a first-rate seamstress, was also a fine cook. I especially remember her curried pork and her macaroni pie. When Mommy Dear was extra busy with her sewing and embroidery work, she would tell me what to cook, and I would do it.

On Sundays, we would all go to the beach, and in the afternoon, we'd go for a walk. All the children would go to watch the green monkeys at Mosquito Bay which is now called Oualie Beach.

Soon, Mommy Dear became the mother for the whole village of Cotton Ground. I remember we had a cousin named Oldain Daniel who often came to our house. One time, we were going to have a beach party, but Oldain didn't have bathing trunks. So Mommy Dear said, "Oldain, I am going to make trunks for you." And she did! Many years after Mommy Dear's death Oldain still remembers that my mother was not only ours, she was also his adopted Mom.

My grandparents, George and Josephine Tyson, were farmers, and often on Sundays, they would kill a rooster, and we'd all enjoy cock soup as a change from our every day staple, rice and peas. I remember, too, that on Sundays, Mommy Dear would pull out the hand crank ice cream maker, and we would all delight in this mouth-watering treat. We sometimes had vanilla, but my favorite was always frozen custard. Yum!

Mommy Dear did some baking in an outside oven fashioned from a 45-gallon drum, a device many folks used in those days. From time to time, my grandparents would kill a pig, and, after rubbing the flesh with salt and pepper, they would spread it in the sun to dry.

Yes, I have many memories of the tastes and smells of those years. There were herbs such as lemongrass and basil; breads and cakes made from cassava meal; johnnycake and goats milk; beverage water that was ordinary water sweetened with cane sugar; and roasted coconuts.

The old women, like my grandmother, who was a bush doctor, swore that the foul-tasting bush teas such as washerwoman or cattle tongue were good for what ails you. One I did like was cinnamon bush tea, and I still drink a lot of it today. To clear out your innards, they made castor oil. If you had a cold, they rubbed your head with coconut oil.

CHAPTER V

I came from the poorest of the poor, yet somehow I knew, or at least felt, that if everyone worked hard, things would get better. I saw Aunt Rose straining to keep her garden producing even in her nineties. I saw Mommy Dear working her fingers to the bone stitching and sewing and mending all hours of the day and night. And this made me want to help out too.

At an early age, I would search for limes, sugar apples and mangoes in the bush. The best place to pick wild limes was Tower Hill. I didn't have to climb the trees--I could get the higher ones down with a hook stick. On a good day, I would gather fifty pounds or so. If I had a donkey along, I'd put the sack on his back. Otherwise, I'd carry the sack on my head.

Monkeys were not a problem in those days. They didn't trouble people because my uncle, Ben France, had a long-range gun and he would shoot all monkeys who came near his village. Lots of people also had a dog to scare off the pests. Many people ate monkey meat, but I never was interested in it.

On Fridays, I would go over to St. Kitts to sell my limes on the sidewalk in Basseterre. Believe me, it was hot sitting in the sun all day long! My favorite spot was across the street from Mrs. Kawaja's supermarket. I didn't really have any regular customers. I just sold what I could to passersby.

There were other boys selling fruit as well, but we weren't really competitors. To the contrary, we helped each other out as much as we could by offering to sell each other's remaining fruit once one or more of us sold out. I'd bundle five or six limes and sell them for four EC cents.

Sometimes Mrs. Kawaja or another supermarket person would come over and buy my whole bag of limes. That day I would go home with ten dollars instead of the usual two. I never had a problem with someone stealing my fruit or my money. In those days, such things just didn't happen.

When I had leftover limes at the end of the day, I'd take them to Lillie Brazier, the daughter of my Great-aunt Frances. Lillie's real name was Rosamond Pemberton. She was married to a chicken farmer who sometimes would give me a dressed chicken to take back to Nevis. Lillie was the organist for the Methodist Church in Basseterre. She was really good at it.

Well, anyway, Lillie had a shop downtown, and she would take the limes I hadn't sold and market them in her shop. She would give me any money she had collected the following week. That way I didn't have to carry limes back to Nevis.

When I went to St. Kitts to sell my limes and mangoes, I used to buy popcorn kernels over there and bring them back to Nevis. On Sundays, I would pop the corn and then go door to door and sell it to the children. I usually crossed over to St. Kitts on one of the ferries, the *MV Christena* or the *MV Silopana*.

The fare in those days was 25 cents one way for children. Since I nearly always missed the last crossing back to Nevis, I would have to return on a lighter, those small sailing vessels folks used to use to transport freight and passengers around the islands. If I was lucky, I would catch the boat owned by Samuel Taylor whose wife was a cousin of my family.

Samuel had two lighters, the *Unity I* and the *Unity II*. He plied the waters between Mosquito Bay and Jones Bay. He docked at a wooden pier, and I was always afraid I'd fall through the spaces between the boards. When I caught a ride with him, I rode for free thus increasing my day's profits which I used to buy food and household goods for Mommy Dear.

More than once I was stuck having to walk back to Cotton Ground in total darkness. But I did it because although I was still very much a youngster, I was on my way to being the man of the family. I fell into this role because my older brothers, the ones still at home, did nothing to help out Mommy Dear. So I did what I could to keep the family fed.

Mommy Dear did her share as well. Continuing to work as a seamstress, she and a niece, Elvira Lescott, found employment with an American lady, Betty Roby. Ms. Roby had a clothing shop in Charlestown across the street from the Anglican Church. Mommy Dear and Elvira were employed to make apparel to sell in the shop which was called Caribbee Clothes.

As I got older, I started taking on numerous odd jobs. I began my career as a landscaper at the home of Bassett and Liz Ferguson, a couple from the United States, whose daughter hired me and my brothers to care for their grounds. The Fergusons, seeing what a hard worker I was, appointed me supervisor of the grounds crew even though I was younger than Alex and Patrick who never were go-getters.

Although I was certainly not aware of it at the time, it probably was a good thing that Mommy Dear placed me with Aunt Rose for I am sure that, in part, my energy and industriousness are due to the fine example she provided when I was of an impressionable age.

In the summertime, I worked up in Cades Bay planting cottonseeds for a dollar a day. The girls dug the holes with a hoe. The boys put nine or ten seeds in a hole. As time passed, we had to go back and thin out the seedlings. I also worked for Fred Clark, Sr. picking up coconuts that were dried out on roof tops to make copra (dried coconut meat) for export to Dominica.

I rode on a donkey cart as a guy named Toby gathered up the unhusked fruit, and then we set up an assembly line of sorts to prepare the juicy white flesh for drying. Toby and Oliver husked the coconuts. I liked to drink the refreshing coconut water. I got 75 cents a day for this work.

When I was still a young boy, one of my relatives asked me to get her some gineps. I climbed a tree, and, when I was some 30 feet up, the branch broke, and I went crashing to the ground. The impact knocked me unconscious, but luckily Mommy Dear heard my fall and came to my rescue. She quickly mixed up a potion of aloe and egg white which I was made to swallow after I came to in the belief that it would clear out any bruised blood cells.

Sometimes I took the ferry over to St. Kitts and got a job carrying rocks in a quarry. Man, that was hard and heavy work! It was a lot easier to pick up golf balls on the old course near the St. Kitts airport. They only paid me 25 cents a day for the balls I collected, but I guess it was worth it.

I remember an old man in my village whose name was Mr. Paul. For a time, he rented a house from my Godmother. Everyone called him "Gerrat" because he was from Antigua, and that is the nickname we Nevisians have traditionally given to folks from that island.

Mr. Paul had lived in the Dominican Republic for a while, and when he came to Nevis, he brought his Dominican girlfriend and her three daughters with him. This relationship didn't last, so the girlfriend and her three daughters moved out.

After the Dominicans left, Mr. Paul met a girl named Jessie, a mulata from Cotton Ground. She was light-skinned due to her white ancestors.

Even though he was no youngster, Mr. Paul was a ladies man. So he got hooked up with Jessie. She was the quiet type who practiced Christian teachings. In her later years, she went blind, and one of my aunts on my father's side had to care for her.

Mr. Paul was very skillful. He farmed his lands and sold honey to earn a living. He worked for me for some time tilling the soil in my gardens with a pitchfork. But as he advanced in age, he was only able to work an eighth of an acre for himself. The result was that he had so little to eat that he had to dig his potatoes before they were ripe. Soon, he was unable to pay his rent, and he had to go to the poorhouse.

When I was going to school in the 70's, the population of Nevis was some 15,000 inhabitants. I remember that it went up to about 17,000 at one time. People had very large families. There were a lot more older people in our village, over a hundred in their 90's and at least ten persons over 100 years of age. In those days, three or four generations lived under the same roof. I had three great-aunts living together in the village of Fountain. My father also had two aunts who had been living in the same house since they were children. They stayed there until they passed away at a great age.

People on this island never had much, but to survive, they shared whatever they had with the family. The main source of food was the crops of bananas and cassava. Both plants can grow all year round and cassava doesn't need a lot of water.

Bananas and sweet potatoes do better from October to December. They produce very well during that time of year, and they are better tasting as well.

Cassava can be cooked as a vegetable, but it can also be ground to make flour which is used to make cassava bread. A couple of my favorite dishes while I was growing up were cassava meal porridge and cassava masa. Cassava masa is made by soaking the cassava meal the way you soak corn meal. Then the masa is baked. It is normally served with steamed fish or stewed liver. The people of Nevis survived on this diet during the years of World War II.

You might ask why the people in Nevis had so many children. Well, it was not easy raising so many children. My Great-grandmother had 13 children. Children, in those days, were our investment for old age. There was no Social Security in St. Kitts and Nevis until 1978. What the country used to have was a providence scheme. The Government would take five percent of your earnings. When you reached age 62, you would get back the money withheld in a lump sum.

Thankfully, the late Premier Bradshaw began a program of Social Security. It was further developed by the administrations which have followed him. We now have a Social Security Pension Plan so that when a person on St. Kitts or Nevis reaches 62, or if they become disabled, they can benefit from the taxes taken from their hard-earned money. Before this program was in place, people had to work as long as they were able.

If you were poor, you had to struggle in your Golden Years to survive. What the people used to do was to raise lots of animals so that when their children got to be young adults, they would sell many of their animals and use the money to send their children abroad in hopes that when the children were overseas, they would send back money to support their parents in their old age. That way they could live with dignity and not have to wait for handouts or go to the Poor House in Charlestown or the Infirmary on St. Kitts.

Now the Poor House is called the Home for the Aged. If you don't have anyone to care for you, you can retire in the Home for the Aged. Those who have any assets must turn them over to the Government. Those who are indigent will be cared for in a special wing reserved for them. We have two of these homes on Nevis, and both are well run. St. Kitts has two homes also. The homes provide health care around the clock.

When I was growing up, most of us had to take care of our old folks. Sometimes, these old people were no relation, but out of love in our hearts, we took care of them.

I had two neighbors, Mr. and Mrs. William, across the street from me, and I used to go to help them just as I would help my grandparents. I chopped wood for their cooking stove. They couldn't manage to do much chopping because of their age. And when the weather was dry, I would go miles to bring buckets of water on my head to assist them. These old folks are no longer with us, but they left me lots of blessings.

My next-door neighbor's name was Florence Jones. We used to call her "Queen" Jones. She was born on the 21st of April, the same birthday as our Queen Elizabeth II. Every year, at the same time in June, Queen Elizabeth celebrates her birthday. Queen Jones also used to have a party.

She had an oven made out of a 45-gallon oil drum in which she would sometimes bake 40 cakes along with about 12 plates of the pastries we called coconut tarts. The filling was ground coconut mixed with sugar. The crust would be filled with the coconut and sugar and then baked for about 30 minutes in the drum oven.

Then she would butcher two goats and make what we in St. Kitts and Nevis call goat water. It is really goat stew made with breadfruit, onions, green pepper, garlic, whole cloves, black pepper, lots of tomato paste and seasoned with lots of herbs to give it a good flavor. After cooking all of that, Queen Jones would bake two hams and slice them. What a party!

But the most important thing about Queen Jones was what she did for the poor and shut-ins in my village. She prepared foods and some other neighborhood children and I were asked to take cake, tarts, goat water and ham to the old and disabled people every Queen's Birthday until Queen Jones became old and no longer able to carry on her tradition. What surprised me about Queen was that she would take people in and care for them even if they were no relation of hers.

Queen was not the only person who would help others, but she did more than all the others put together. She used to bring me hand-me-down clothing from St. Croix for which I was very appreciative. But I remember she brought me several pairs of white pants, so I went to town and bought some cheap dye to color them up a bit.

Sometimes, her children would get upset, but Queen would never give up. She helped people until she got on in age and could no longer do it. I am sure she will be rewarded in Heaven. She touched so many lives, many of whom have gone on to the Great Beyond.

Well, Queen took ill in January of 1999 and went to the nursing home where she passed away. The nurse reported that Queen's last words were, "I have asked the Lord to forgive me, and nothing is better than being with Jesus." Queen died on June 5, 1999 at 82 years of age. She had a good life of kindness and loving others as she loved herself.

In my village we had some four bakers. All of them baked in stone ovens. Those who couldn't afford a stone oven baked in a 45-gallon drum or an oil pan which they placed over a burning coal pot. Most working people in those days would buy one bag of flour which was expected to last a month. Many people raised animals. Milk from goats and cows was also available.

At night, the young people in my village would make a flambeau by putting lamp oil in a bottle. We would take the lights to go crabbing. We would sell all the land crabs we could catch to an old man called Papa France. He paid us 60 cents a dozen, and then he would ship them off Island. We had to catch quite a lot of crabs to make any money!

Sometimes, Mommy Dear would go crabbing with us. I always liked it when she came along because it seemed like we caught more crabs when she was there. We were also happy because we loved her, and we wanted her to take a break from that pedal-operated sewing machine where she worked from morning to night trying to make ends meet.

We also had to till the land. Most young people had to work on the land before they left for school. I believe that this hard work made the kids of my generation tough. We were trained from an early age to work hard, to be honest, to respect our elders, and to always tell the truth no matter what. In my day, this is how all the children in my village were raised.

I remember that Mommy Dear would beat me if I came home later than I was supposed to. But I wasn't the only one. She beat us all, even one of my brothers who was in his late teens. He complained, saying that he was a man and shouldn't be beaten. Mommy Dear's reply was that she was the only adult in the family and that her word was law!

And so, that was my life, with me and Mommy Dear trying our best to keep the family afloat. Those last four years when Mommy Dear was with us (1966-1970) were tough financially, but she always made sure that all of her children had enough to eat.

I don't know how she did it. I only know I did what I could to help out. I don't really know what would have become of me if nothing out of the ordinary had ever happened. But one day something extraordinary did happen, and my life was changed forever.

CHAPTER VI

I have learned that life is full of mysteries and unanswered questions. I know that people throughout the ages have tried to explain things that they can't understand in all kinds of ways. The ones who foolishly try to be objective chalk up events they can't explain to pure chance. And yet, I cannot help but wonder if perhaps there is another explanation, one that would take us one step beyond, into the unknown.

I recall vividly the night of July 28, 1970. It was a Tuesday, and I was asleep in the living room when Mommy Dear came up to me and shook me awake. "Ozzie," she said, "can you see that bright light?" It was as dark as always at night. I couldn't see my hand in front of my face. We had no current in the house.

I thought she had gone mad, but I just said, "No, Mommy Dear, I don't see anything."

Mommy Dear heaved a painful sigh and said, "Ozzie, I'm going to die. Your brother, Clyde, will take care of you."

The next day, Mommy Dear and my brothers, Dave and Kirsten, took the ferry to St. Kitts. Mommy Dear had been engaged to do last minute alterations to a bridal gown she had made for the bride-to-be of her second cousin, Winston Ives. I had seen the dress while Mommy Dear was making it. It was milky white and had lace to go around the bride's face. The wedding was planned for Thursday.

Mommy Dear and my brothers were going to stay with Mommy Dear's favorite niece, Violet Donovan, while on St. Kitts.

At the time, I was caring for a neighbor lady, Ellen Etilinda Henry. She was a businesswoman of East Indian descent who owned a large tract of land next to my family's lot. Mrs. Henry had been paralyzed from the waist down as the result of a freak accident.

She was on her way to St. Kitts in 1934 on a sailing vessel. While passing under the spar of the ship, it broke off and fell on her hitting her spine just under her neck. Some folks say that someone had put an obeah curse on her as no one had ever heard of a similar accident. Due to her injuries, she never recovered use of her legs. That's why I was helping her out.

I did all kinds of jobs for her. I brought her water; I helped her to cook on a coal pot next to her bed; I brought her tubs of water and her dirty clothes so she could wash them. She even made me take care of her bedpans. Can you imagine? I waited on her hand and foot, and she treated me very well. I never heard her complain about being crippled. She never paid me. I didn't care. It was a labor of love.

Since Mommy Dear had gone to St. Kitts, I spent the next two nights at Mrs. Henry's house. On Thursday night, I dreamt that I had missed the boat to St. Kitts that I was planning to take the next morning. My dream proved to be prophetic for I overslept and missed the morning ferry. I had no choice but to wait for the afternoon crossing.
I hitched a ride to town with a fella name of Benson Jones, and I boarded the *MV Christena* at 5:00PM on Friday afternoon.

The *MV Christena* was a two-decker, partially enclosed craft. I had crossed on her frequently on my way to sell limes in Basseterre. She was in poor repair, and she always took on water in the lower level. If I had worn shoes, the water would have ruined them as it came up to my ankles.

Anyway, on that day I made it to Basseterre as usual and went to the home of Viola Griffin, the daughter of the woman I was caring for on Nevis. I served as a courier between Mrs. Henry and her daughter. I carried notes back and forth and took meat and cooked food to Mrs. Henry.

Mrs. Griffin was a seamstress and a friend of Mommy Dear. She was married to an elderly butcher whom folks called "Yankee" since he had spent a lot of time in the States. He always wore a jacket and a tie, at least when I saw him.

I still remember what a good baker Mrs. Griffin was. Her black cake was absolutely delicious!

So I spent the night at Mrs. Griffin's home, and on Saturday morning, I headed for my spot on the sidewalk across from Mrs. Kawaja's market to sell the limes and mangoes I had collected in the bush on Nevis. On Saturday afternoon, I went to meet up with Mommy Dear and my brothers for the return to Nevis.

CHAPTER VII

Saturday, August 1, 1970, was Emancipation Day, a celebration to commemorate the ending of slavery in the British Empire in 1838. So lots of folks were returning to Nevis to spend the holiday as well as to see the horse races on Sunday.

Among the many people milling around the Treasury Pier waiting to board the *MV Christena*, I saw my second cousin, Anita Jones, who was visiting from St. Croix. She was a beautiful woman, a mixture of African and Indian features. I couldn't understand why she was dressed all in black with a long black dress and black shoes.

It was much later that I learned the story. She had been visiting her family in Fountain, and that morning, as she prepared to leave for St. Kitts, she had dressed all in black. As she stood in front of a floor-length mirror, she announced to her family, as Mommy Dear had done to me four days earlier, "I am going to die."

I cannot help but wonder what these women knew and how they could have known it. I guess the answers to my questions will remain forever in the twilight zone.

So we're all on Treasury Pier waiting for departure, me, Mommy Dear, my brothers, Dave and Kirsten, and my half-sister, Anita Liburd. Anita had come over to St. Kitts that morning to collect money owed to her grandmother--and mine too--for charcoal she had sold and sent over on the ferry. Anita was very obedient and completely trustworthy.

I liked Anita very much, better than my brothers. I used to go up to see her and my grandmother when I could. Anita would help me look for fruit in the bush.

Anyway, we were about to get on board the *MV Christena* when I saw Adelpha Maynard come up to the boat with her little girl. She handed the child down to a passenger on board and asked her to bring the girl to her grandmother on Nevis where she would spend the rest of the summer. I also saw men loading lots of bags of potatoes and breadfruit on the ferry.

All of us got on board. Mommy Dear, Dave and Kirsten took seats on the lower level toward the middle. Anita and I went to sit near the opening at the back. Anita had a piece of cake with white frosting. She offered me half. She was such a sweet girl. Then she turned to me suddenly and said, "Brother, if this boat sinks, I'm going to drown." I didn't like to hear people talking spooks. I felt a lump in my throat as I heard these words.

The *MV Christena* took off before the scheduled departure time of 3:30PM. She was extremely overloaded with passengers--more than twice what she was designed to carry. As the boat took off, Captain Ponteen passed through the cabin, singing as he collected the fares he expected to pocket, "Come, leh we go, Suki," a calypso song popular at the time.

We hadn't gone far when a good-sized wave sent the water creeping up around my knees, and I knew something was wrong. The boat was sitting deep in the water and was rocking in a strange way.

Suddenly, one of the engines cut out, I guess due to flooding. About a mile off Nags Head, that horse-like promontory which reaches toward the Caribbean at the extreme western end of St. Kitts' Southern Peninsula, the stern of the *MV Christena* went under, her wide bow went up in the air, and the vessel was on its way to the depths. I lost sight of Anita and never saw her again.

CHAPTER VIII

There were some 218 jackets on board, some stored in the Captain's cabin and the rest in nets overhead in the passenger sections. They are hard to access even under the best of conditions, but with the *MV Christena* tipped up in a vertical position, it was nearly impossible. A few, including my cousin, Hensley Colbourne, were able to get one out and survive. There were also five buoyant seat cushions, but somehow they got lodged inside the vessel and were therefore of no use.

Luckily, I had learned to swim some years before when a neighbor lady dragged me out to sea near Nelson's Spring and let me go. It was either sink or swim so swim I did. After that, I spent a lot of time swimming in the sea with my friends.

So, when I found myself under water, I immediately thrust myself up and made my way clear of the sinking boat. I could see the shore was too far away for me to attempt to reach it. I paddled around, grabbing on to anything that was floating, pretty much in a state of shock.

The teachers had taught us to recite Psalm 107 at St. Thomas School, so I kept repeating a section of it time after time as my prayer to be saved.

> *They that go down to the sea in ships,*
> *that do business in great waters;*
> *these see the works of the Lord,*
> *and his wonders in the deep.*
> *For He commandeth, and raiseth the stormy wind,*
> *which lifteth up the waves thereof.*

They mount up to the heaven,
they go down again to the depths;
their soul is melted because of trouble.
They reel to and fro,
and stagger like a drunken man,
and are at their wit's end.
Then they cry unto the Lord in their trouble,
and he bringeth them out of their distresses.
He maketh the storm a calm,
so that the waves thereof are still.
Then they are glad because they be quiet;
so that he bringeth them unto their desired haven.
Oh, that men would praise the Lord for his goodness,
and for his wonderful works to the children of men!

I saw bodies floating everywhere. The water around me was stained with blood. I guess a lot of people must have got cut or bruised as they struggled to get free of the boat. The blood attracted the sharks. They had never bothered anyone before, that I had heard of, but on this day the sharks came like monkeys to a mango tree.

I heard people screaming and wailing. I saw Mommy Dear's suitcase floating by. Then, a sight I'll never forget, my little brother Kirsten floating face down, already dead. I was wearing brand new leather shoes that Mommy Dear had just bought for me in St. Kitts. I tried desperately to get them off so that I could swim better, but I just couldn't do it.

CHAPTER IX

I was scared and alone, wondering what was to become of me when my prayers were answered. Jesus had not forsaken me. A small boat, owned by my uncle, Desmond Tyson, was returning from a trip to St. Kitts where the crew had gone to sell fish. They happened upon the disaster and began picking up survivors. Among the folks they had already rescued was Diana, the daughter of Mrs. Williams who owned the grocery store on Main Street in Charlestown.

Along with her was a fella name of Joseph Martin. He had asked the captain of the fishing boat, Peter "Turkey" Maynard, to please find his grandson. While they were searching for the young man, they spotted me and pulled me aboard. I collapsed on the floor of the boat. I immediately noticed that there was a woman on board, known to me as Luella Budgeon, who had a big gash on her forehead which was bleeding profusely. With no concern for modesty, she took off her knickers and used them to stop the flow of blood.

Soon, the crew spotted Mike Martin, and they pulled him aboard. Although there were many voices clamoring to be rescued, the Captain decided not to risk another disaster by overloading his small craft. He headed full speed for Pinney's Beach and did not to return to the scene after the rescued parties had been dumped ashore.

I guess it was because "Turkey" saw the *Sea Hunter* take off at high speed from Cliff Dwellers with Captain Alphonse Skeete in command. It was a much larger and much faster boat and was able to pick up the remaining survivors.

Being the most agile of the rescued passengers, I ran ahead along Pinney's Beach in Charlestown. I was wearing long pants and a striped blue shirt Mommy Dear had just made for me. The first person I met, Wentworth Nicholls, owner of the Pinney Beach Hotel, would not believe my report that the *MV Christena* had gone down and that lots of people had died. He told me I was crazy.

I didn't know what to do to let people know what had happened. The first person to believe me was Christian Atherton, the Water Supervisor. He broke into tears when I gave him the news. The people in Charlestown had been watching the *MV Christena's* arrival, when all of a sudden she disappeared.

Mr. Atherton took me to the Police Station where I gave a full report of the disaster. The police, in turn, noting that I was in a state of shock, took me to the hospital. I was indeed traumatized, "out of it" as we say today.

As I was lying in my hospital bed, a guy named Toby--his real name was Milford Queen--called me over to the window and said, "Look, Ozzie, see the last of your mother!" I had to look though fearing what I would see. To be sure, I immediately recognized Mommy Dear's green dress, one that she had made herself, of course. They were carrying her into the hospital on a stretcher. I wondered how I was going to make it without Mommy Dear.

Mommy Dear was dead. Anita was dead. Dave was dead. Kirsten was dead. Kirsten was my favorite brother. I still dream about him sometimes. His tragic death is so sad. So many good people lost their lives. Sometimes I wonder why. Only God knows. He is the answer to all our prayers. We must not question Him.

CHAPTER X

Everyone in the hospital was crying and sobbing as they watched the men bring in truckloads of the drowned victims. The nurses told me that people had driven to the airport that night and lit up the runway with their headlights so that planes bringing supplies and personnel from Puerto Rico could land. I learned later that most, if not all, of the 259 bodies recovered were buried in an unmarked mass grave in the Stoney Grove Cemetery on Sunday.

The bodies of my brothers and my dear little half-sister were never found. As time passed, I was told that Mommy Dear had not drowned. Apparently, the medical exam showed that she had died from a heart attack--there was no water in her lungs. I can only hope that her end was so quick that she did not have to struggle in a state of panic.

There have been many myths, which have risen up regarding the sinking of the *MV Christena*. The most common one is that for some reason the passengers all rushed to one side--some say to escape the rain--hardly necessary in an enclosed vessel, not to mention that it was a clear day--and because of the overload, the boat tipped over sideways.

The fact is it did not tip over. The stern went down first. I have been told that there is an explanation for this. An investigation of the disaster revealed that welders from the St. Kitts sugar factory had been repairing the exhaust system the day before.

When the welders left, they apparently failed to secure the bulkhead manholes, and the crew apparently did not check up on this. It is hypothesized that since the *MV Christena* always took on water in the bilge as a matter of course, giving the water free access to the bottom rear compartment made the stern go down, under such excess weight.

Experts have calculated that had those manholes been properly closed, the *MV Christena* could have limped to Charlestown even with its grossly overloaded cargo of passengers. Sadly, we will never know. (Readers who would like more details of the sinking can consult *The Christena Disaster Revisited* by Whitman T. Browne, St. Thomas: BL & E Enterprises, 2000)

The doctor from Puerto Rico who examined me in the hospital said I had a strong nerve. I guess this is so. Family members wanted me to go to live with my uncle. But I knew that he was a heavy drinker and a gambler, and I just didn't want to be in his house.

At the time of the *MV Christena* disaster my Grandmother Tyson had already died and my Grandmother Liburd didn't want to take me in. I suppose it was because she had no income and was dependent on what little support she could get from her children. So I went back to take care of Mrs. Henry who was happy to have me.

CHAPTER XI

On Tuesday night, three days after the *MV Christena* went down, I was sleeping on the floor in Mrs. Henry's hallway with just a pillow and a blanket, as she had no bedroom for me. Suddenly, I felt someone tugging on my blanket. I looked around and could see no one.

I knew it couldn't be Mrs. Henry as she was paralyzed and immobile without help. I had heard that the dead will rise after three days, so I am certain that it was Mommy Dear's spirit who had come to see if I was all right. I guess she was satisfied that I would be cared for as she never came back again.

When my father heard of my loss, he sent £5 from England via his mother, my grandmother, Hilda Archibald. I never heard from him again. At times I thought I might like to meet him, but even though in later life I could have gone to England to look him up, I decided not to do so.

I guess I should also mention that even though the *MV Christena* was a government- operated ferry, I never got one penny of compensation. This in spite of the fact that on August 2, 1970, Deputy Premier C.A. Paul Southwell announced the formation of the *MV Christena* Disaster Fund. I heard that a few people got grants, administered by the Anglican priest, Cannon Blant, but others, such as Orlando Brown, who also lost his mother, and I, got nothing.

The *MV Christena* survivors have never really met as a group though some of us do see each other at the memorial service held each August 1st at the memorial monument in Charlestown.

The spirit of my dear half-sister, Anita, stayed with me quite a while. From time to time, I would walk up to Fountain to see my paternal grandmother, and on the way back to Cotton Ground, I would hear footsteps on the track behind me. When I turned to look, there was never anyone there. I am sure that Anita was following me because she missed me so much.

While I was living with Mrs. Henry, I worked the land for her and cultivated her small garden in addition to caring for her needs in the house. Much to my chagrin, after about a year, one of Mrs. Henry's daughters, Elsie, who, by the way, was a heavy drinker, came to Nevis from England and forced me to leave the place. She wasn't good to her mother either.

So I went to live in Charlestown with my uncle, Charles Tyson, and his wife, Rose. Uncle Charles worked on a lighter, and Rose worked in the hospital kitchen. They were caring for eleven children in their home at that time. While I was there, I got a job cleaning Arthur Evelyn's office, and I also did odd jobs for Estella Myers who had a shop on Craddock Road. I developed a good relationship with the clergymen on Nevis, and I was lucky to get work with three or four of them doing odd jobs such as washing their cars, polishing their floors, or feeding their chickens.

I attended school at St. Thomas but not regularly as I couldn't afford to buy books and other materials. I became known as a storyteller, and sometimes the teacher would call me to the head of the class to recite.

My stories were usually about jumbies, but they were true stories of what actually happened to people I knew or had heard about. I can't remember the ones I actually told in school, but I'll give you a couple of examples of stories I've heard since.

There was a man walking to Mt. Lily on a path cut through the bush. He saw that a rainstorm was coming up fast so he ducked under a tree for protection. As he leaned against the tree, he passed gas. Much to his surprise he heard a voice cry out, "Hey, mon, you just flattered on me!"

Well, they say that revenge is sweet. Not long after, this same man had arranged to meet a certain woman in the bush. All of a sudden, he saw her. She was very pretty, but somehow she looked different from the woman he was expecting to meet. Mindful of that old saying about a bird in the hand, the man began to undress the young lady.

Strangely, each time he removed an article of her clothing, another layer would appear in its place. The puzzled man happened to look down at his partner's feet and discovered not dainty toes but rather goat hooves! When he looked up, her beautiful face had turned into that of a goat. You can imagine that the jumbie thought it was a lot funnier than the man did!

I'd heard a lot of Anancy stories as well. I remember that one about Anancy getting inside the cattle and eating the meat from the inside out.

People also tell a lot of ghost stories. An old lady who lived in my neighborhood was always friendly to me. I knew her for many years and took to calling her Mommy. She used to give me Ovaltine which I loved! She was always well-dressed but there was one odd thing about her. She let a chicken nest in her bed, and the chicken actually laid her eggs right there!

Well, anyway, she told me that one night after her husband had died, she went to close up the shutters. As she reached out to grab one she felt cold clammy hands on top of hers. Her dead husband had come back to help her, but instead, he scared her out of her wits!

Well, you may not believe in ghost stories, but I do. When I was living for a while up in Waterbury, Connecticut, the house I was staying in was evidently haunted. I'd hear strange noises all night long, but when I heard a door slam, I'd get up to investigate but never find anyone there. I learned later that an old guy had died in the house some years before. Apparently he wanted us to know that at least part of him never left.

A neighbor told me that she had lived in a house where a murder took place. At a certain time each year, blood would start dripping from the ceiling. People would check the flooring above and find nothing. After a while she was so upset she moved out.

I was later told that the whole residential area had been built on land formerly used as a cemetery. I wonder if some of those disrupted spirits are now wandering around. At times, we would act out the stories by each taking a part.

CHAPTER XII

I stayed with Uncle Charles for about two years. When I started working at Cliff Dwellers, the McDonalds made a room for me at the hotel.

I began working as a bar helper for Carol McDonald who was manager of Cliff Dwellers Hotel. I washed glasses and learned how to mix drinks. When the oil embargo in the early 70's cut off Cliff Dwellers' supply of cooking gas, I made an oven out of an oil drum. Claudina Pinney, the hotel's head cook, used it like a coal pot to cook desserts, bread and soup. It kept the kitchen going for quite a while!

Carol took an interest in me and saw to it that I attended school regularly. St. Thomas was still an all-age school. I remember there was one bully who troubled a lot of us. His name was Jack Rogers. His father was a sea captain--no relation to Jolly Roger as far as I know! Anyway, this guy, who was tall and quite strong, once hit me over the head and did a number on me.

I loved to read. I had learned to read at the Catholic School in Basseterre. I'd go to the library in Charlestown to find books. Then I met a teacher from the United States, Mrs. McFadden, and after she learned of my interest, she brought me books as did Mr. Bud Verdier who took a liking to me.

Oddly, his brother, Alfred, was a good friend of mine. He was what they call today "intellectually challenged", but to us he was just a slow learner. So the teacher would say to me, "Ozzie, you take Alfred and a couple of other boys, and you teach them the lesson." So I did as best I could. For many years after that Alfred always called me "teacher".

   My favorite teacher was Mrs. Powell. The Principal, Mrs. Byron, was a tyrant who beat the children with a leather strap if they arrived late. One time she got my shirt all bloody. Nonetheless, I managed to finish grade twelve. I liked school for the most part, and, in general, I was well behaved.

   You know, it's funny. Everybody thought Dave and Kirsten were real smart, and they were. My older brothers thought I was stupid because I was more interested in hard work than in limin'.

   When we did sports, I was very good as a long distance runner. And speaking of running reminds me that I got myself two donkeys that I used to race. I named them Jenny and Kicker. We used to have races down by the pool below Cliff Dwellers every Sunday. Afterward we would have fried chicken and hot dogs.

   In addition to weekday school. I also attended Sunday School regularly. We learned Bible stories about all the Old Testament heroes, and we also memorized certain verses.

In 1973, I returned to the family home in Cotton Ground to live with my oldest brother, Clyde. Since he had been living off island pretty much since my birth, I had only met him for the first time a short while before. Clyde was rough and tough with me and didn't help me out at all. I was completely on my own.

Luckily, my uncle, Carleton Tyson, helped me out by giving me fish and arranging for credit at the local grocery shop so that I could buy rice and other basics.

In 1974, a terrible drought hit Nevis bringing on a serious economic crisis. Everyone had to struggle to survive. Nothing would grow it was so dry. I couldn't find any limes in the bush to sell. I'd go down to the fishermen's beaches and help them to haul their boats in or out. In return, they'd give me a couple of fish.

Sometimes I'd eat them, and sometimes I'd sell one or two so I could buy some rice or flour. I struggled, using my wits and creativity. I survived.

CHAPTER XIII

When I was sixteen, I began taking care of the house owned by Americans Charles and Jane Smith. I worked for them year round for five years. When they sold to Rod Prendergast, a guy from Boston, I only stayed on for a few months. His wife was real nice, but that guy had a real attitude problem. He was continually talking down to me as if I was his slave.

I have to say that as a young man quite often other guys were interested in the same girls who attracted me. I never was willing to fight for a girl's affection. I figured if she didn't like me, there was no point in trying to win her over. This feeling is still with me today. I know some guys spend lots of money on women they want to impress, but that's not my style.

I tell the women who I am, and, if they like me, fine. If they don't, I move on. Though I am sort of a solitary type, I am not bashful. I find it easy to talk with women, and this helps me to find out what's on their mind. Sometimes the mothers of the girls I was interested in would try to interfere. Mothers are the same everywhere. They want their daughters to marry rich guys and stay away from those who are considered unworthy. I guess I can understand this as I want the best for my daughters too.

I progressed through the ranks while working at Cliff Dwellers and finally became a bartender. I concocted a special drink called Fanny's Folly for the bartenders" contest the Island held in 1987 as part of the Nelson/Nisbett Bicentennial celebrations. It was made with dark rum, pineapple and orange juice, limes, Angostura bitters, grenadine and ginger--all ingredients that would have been available on the Island in 1787.

I also served a lot of Cliff Hangers which were sort of the official drink of the hotel. This was a strong drink made with lots of rum, fresh ginger, pineapple juice, and a few other ingredients.

Since I was only hired during the high season, the rest of the year I had to look for landscaping work. I remember that I worked for Bobbie Wilson for a while. She was very strict, wanting me to do several things at once or start a new job before the old one was finished. But I liked her just the same.

In 1980, David Myers, the owner of Cliff Dwellers Hotel told me, "Ozzie, I put two hundred thousand US dollars into this hotel. That's more money than you'll ever see."

Given my humble beginnings, that might have been a reasonable prediction. But I recalled the words of US President Woodrow Wilson.

> "We grow great by dreams. All big men are dreamers. They see things in the soft haze of a spring day or in the red fire of a long winter's evening. Some of us let these great dreams die, but others nourish and protect them, nurse them through bad days 'til they bring them to the sunshine and light which comes always to those who sincerely hope that their dreams will come true."

I had dreamt of owning a guesthouse of my own since I was a teenager. I was determined to prove David Myers wrong.

CHAPTER XIV

In 1982, I had gone to St. Croix to find landscaping work. I had a cousin, Samuel Tyson, who lived there. I called him "Uncle" 'cause he was a lot older than me. He was the son of Mommy Dear's oldest sister, Adrilana. Uncle Sam invited me to live with him.

Mommy Dear had always been close to Uncle Sam, so I felt comfortable with him and trusted him. Uncle Sam was good to all the family. He helped me to get landscaping work and taught me to save money. He told me that no matter how little I earned each week, I should put a small part of it away for savings. And you know something? I took his advice. I remembered my dream and kept on making plans for my guesthouse.

In the high season, I'd go back to Nevis to work at Cliff Dwellers. I also started a taxi service with a little Toyota Corolla. I had to study up on Nevis history, take a test and pay $200 for my taxi license. I did pretty well on the test as I've always liked history.

I never have had any really bad experiences as a taxi driver. There are times when I haven't been paid the full fare. I guess sometimes tourists spend more on their trip down here than they expected so they are short of cash when I pick them up. Those who are drunk or grouchy I have learned to deal with by being diplomatic. That keeps me out of trouble.

I continued to work hard both on Nevis and on St. Croix, and I saved as much as I could.

I had told my neighbor, Melvina Sanders, in 1984, that I was going to open a small grocery shop on the family land in Cotton Ground. She said, "Boy, you plumb crazy!" but I got the last laugh. In 1985, I opened my doors and welcomed my first customers. In my one-room shop, equipped with a bar/counter, some stools and a few shelves I sold groceries, chicken, drinks and produce.

Later I set up a bakery in an out-building and made crackers, biscuits and muffins on an oil pan fired by a coal pot. I had no gas burners, so I had to fire up the charcoal every day. I had learned to make muffins while working at Cliff Dwellers. And now I was able to take muffins up to Cliff Dwellers for them to serve to their clients.

People tell me my tannia fritters were among the Island's best. My dream was coming true. That same year my brother Clyde left for Virgin Gorda where he has been ever since.

In 1986, I decided to visit my brother Alex in the States. He lives in Waterbury, Connecticut, but I visited New York City as well, wanting to see my Aunt Alberta who had sent me money every Christmas, the only gifts I ever received. She lived in a nice neighborhood in Mount Vernon, but when I traveled around the Bronx, the garbage and run-down buildings disgusted me.

Waterbury wasn't much better. There were lots of old steel mills. The US economy was in bad shape. I couldn't find work, and I didn't like the cold. I decided that the US has the good, the bad and the ugly.

CHAPTER XV

So back to Nevis I came, and I returned to my old job at Cliff Dwellers. I liked working with Ira Martin who was at that time managing the hotel. I remember one time at Cliff Dwellers we had a guest who was a real troublemaker. He was a short, fat old guy from the US, and he wanted to fight with everybody including the manager. So we decided to kick him out. We got a taxi driver to take him down to Pinney Beach Hotel where we dumped him on Mr. Nicholls.

Things never stay the same. Business in my shop was slow, and I had more and more competition as each week passed. So it was back to St. Croix to take up Ozzie's Landscaping Service once again. Then, in 1989, Hurricane Hugo devastated Cliff Dwellers Hotel as well as doing extensive damage on St. Croix.

You must know by now that I am no quitter. My dream was never far from my thoughts, and I knew the only way to make it come true was to work, work, work. So I did.

I hadn't met a lot of famous people at Cliff Dwellers--though Robert Plant of Led Zeppelin stayed there once--but during the five years I tended bar at Four Seasons I met a few. The four I remember best were George H. W. Bush, who people now call George I; Harry Belafonte; Paul from The Young and the Restless; and Chris Evert Lloyd and her family.

In 1994, I was back on Nevis for a time. While there, I met a woman in the village of Cotton Ground who had come back to Nevis to visit her family. She had been living in the US and had had a daughter, Leslie, in California in 1992.

Well, I took a liking to Leela, and a few months later, we were married. We got married in Cotton Ground, but not long after, we went to St. Croix to live. I returned to my landscaping business, and things went well for a while. My daughter, Theodora, named after Mommy Dear, was born in 1996.

As in most relationships, I had some good times with my wife and daughters. On Sundays, I would take the family to the movies. My little daughter-- we called her Tati--would say to me, "Baby up", and I would carry her riding on my shoulders. She loved that! She also loved to go to the movies, but before the movie was over, she would be fast asleep.

Leslie, my older daughter, never slept in the movies even when she was quite young. Her favorite movies were ghost stories. My younger daughter loved to have Daddy take her shopping. I learned not to take her near the doll section because she would want to take them all home with her. Sometimes, I would get a babysitter and take my wife out on a date, just the two of us.

But Leela and I couldn't make our marriage work. In 2001, we got divorced.

It was a bitter separation. We had numerous custody battles, and the Court awarded Leela the bulk of my assets on St. Croix. The Courts in the Virgin Islands favor the women in divorce cases.

I had a court-appointed attorney who was totally incompetent as far as protecting my interests was concerned. Throughout the years of my marriage I had never wanted my family to break up. The divorce devastated me. It sapped my inner strength. It was my spiritual upbringing that kept me sane.

Although I had managed to stay afloat when the *Christena* sank, this time I felt that I was going to go down. And down I went until I hit rock bottom. I had no wife, no daughters, no home, no money. In the early years after my divorce it was hard to see my daughters, but as they got older, they challenged my ex-wife and demanded to see me.

But that was all a long time ago. I still miss the happy moments. In spite of the issues that separated us, my ex-wife and I remain good friends and in general things are mellow now. My daughters love me and care about me very much, but because of the terms of the divorce, they will remain apart from me forever.

But my advice to young people is that they make every effort to make their marriages work. Breaking up is always painful. Couples should not give up on each other. I believe it is better to stay together than to end up in Heartbreak Hotel like me. Starting over is never easy.

When my family and I parted company, I had to sleep in my car for a while, but once again, some good people came to my rescue. I was reluctant to ask Uncle Samuel for more help.

At the time I was working for my friends, Jefferson and Sarah Sorenson, who had an apartment on the east end of St. Croix. They fixed up their basement for me to stay in.

I got myself back to work as a landscaper, and, after a while, I was able to pay the Sorensons rent for my room. Jeff also lent me some money to buy another car as the one I had was no longer serviceable.

Jeff was a real Christian and a very nice gentleman. He taught me that true friends are more dependable than family when you're down and out. After Jeff was diagnosed with brain cancer, he said to me, "Ozzie, if I don't see you again, I'll see you in Heaven." I never did see Jeff again. He died a couple of weeks later.

I kept my sanity and my hopeful spirit by leaning on Jesus Christ for support. He had helped me to survive the *Christena* disaster, and he helped me to make it through the aftermath of my divorce. And, then, of course, the kindness of others is what helps us all to make it. I am a true believer in that verse from the Barbra Streisand song, "People who need people are the luckiest people in the world!"

After a time, my ex-wife gave up our apartment, and I moved back in. I discovered that she had left no furniture and no household goods of any kind. So, I worked hard at my landscaping business, and, following the advice of Uncle Samuel, I saved as much as I could.

Sometimes, it just seems like the Fates have it in for you. I was in a neighbor's apartment one day. She was a young woman, in her twenties, I would say, very poor, in fact, so poor that she couldn't pay her bills, so they had cut off her electricity. I had gone over to borrow something when her boyfriend came in, pulled out a long knife and held it to my throat.

I had absolutely no romantic interest in this girl, and I guess she convinced him of this fact as he let me go unharmed. I avoided them after that. I had not reported the boyfriend to the police because I had heard of violent retributions against informers. I just wanted to mind my own business and be left alone. I did feel sorry for that poor girl. Her father was an alcoholic, and her two brothers had been murdered in St. Kitts. Nonetheless, I asked her not to come over for water or whatever anymore.

Over on Nevis, I had closed my little shop, so when Gillian Smith asked me if she could rent the space to start up a restaurant she was going to call "Bananas", I agreed. Some time later, she moved her restaurant up to a renovated space on Cliff Dwellers, and I rented my place to a guy who ran a vegetarian restaurant for a while.

Having been able to save up some money, I had a feeling that the time was coming when I could make my dream a reality. I began to design the guesthouse I had in mind. I started construction in 2004.

By 2005, I was ready to go back to Nevis, and, using available credit, I finished construction of my twelve-unit dream: Palm Springs Guest House. It sits proudly on the crest of the little hill which dominates the land my family has owned and worked for five generations. It is painted bright yellow so no one can miss it. You see, David Myers, it can be done! I did it!

CONCLUSION

I'm still interested in history. You may recall that I had to study Nevis history to get my taxi driver's license. But I've also studied the history of the United States because of the close relationship Nevis and the US have had over the centuries. For example, the first settlers who went to Virginia in 1607 came to Nevis from England and spent some time here before moving on to the wilds of North America.

Alexander Hamilton was born in Charlestown, Nevis in 1755 of British parents. His father was a plantation owner who produced sugar on the Hamilton Estate. When hard times came, the Hamiltons set sail for St. Croix in the Danish West Indies. Alexander was only seven years old.

Alexander became a newspaper boy on St. Croix to help out economically. He was a bright young lad. He left St. Croix as a teenager and moved to what is now the United States, intending to study law.

He was successful in becoming a lawyer at an unusually early age. Living in New York, he met a young woman who came from a very well-to-do family. They married, and over the next several years, she bore him eight children.

Alexander also met George Washington and Aaron Burr. Together they fought in the War of Independence to free the colonies from British rule. In 1776, the colonies declared themselves free. This declaration was followed by a long and bitter war in which many souls lost their lives.
     Upon the successful conclusion of the struggle, George Washington became the first President and Alexander Hamilton became Secretary of the Treasury. In fact, Alexander was the one who designed the financial system for the new country. Hamilton also became Secretary of the Army and Accountant General.

     In 1804, Mr. Hamilton engaged in a duel with his political rival, Aaron Burr. Alexander drew his pistol but did not fire. Mr. Burr, sadly, did not reciprocate. He shot and killed Mr. Hamilton leaving his wife to raise the eight children by herself. But she did so and lived to be in her nineties having seen many of her generation pass on before her.

     Some years after Mr. Hamilton left Nevis, the first hotel in the Caribbean was built on Nevis. In 1778, an Englishman, who had fallen in love with the island of Nevis, built the Bath Hotel. The builder not only was impressed by the wealth of Nevis, he was enthusiastic about the hot bath stream. So he decided to build his hotel nearby to enable his guests to take a rejuvenating hot bath without going more than a short distance.

The hotel was very successful. People from all over Europe came to visit the hot baths. For many years, the English used to call the bath stream the "Fountain of Youth" due to the belief that a good soak in the waters would wash the years away.

After so many years, the hot bath stream, which runs from the mountain to the sea, is still used by locals and visitors who come to Nevis. So Nevis has been engaged in the tourist trade for over 332 years, longer than any other country in the Caribbean.

Although I have not involved myself much in Nevisian politics, I am proud of the way our leaders have developed our islands during my lifetime.

Though I am not a political activist, I have followed the actions of our nation's leaders closely due to my love of country and to my interest in history. Here are a few of my thoughts and memories, Dear Reader.

When I was born, St. Kitts and Nevis, along with Anguilla, were united as a colony under the rule of Great Britain as they had been for most of the past 340 years. Because of the desire of the Islanders for self-rule, in 1967, Britain granted them the status of Associated State.

Robert L. Bradshaw, who had been the Association's Chief Minister, became the first Premier. Anguilla was unhappy with the control exercised over them by St. Kitts, so they broke away and returned to direct rule under Great Britain.

Bradshaw, the only child of Mary Jane Francis lived in the village of St. Paul on St. Kitts. He was one of the founding members of the Labor Party. Since Mr. Bradshaw's first run for office, no candidate of another party has ever won a seat in the St. Paul parish. It has been a Labor stronghold for some 55 years.

Robert L. Bradshaw is considered the Father of the country because when the islands were in darkness, he brought electric power to St. Kitts and Nevis. This was crucial for the development of the country. Bradshaw was the champion of the poor.

He helped to create labor unions so that working men and women could have a voice and thus improve their working conditions. Bradshaw was also the first leader to start the construction of better homes that would be affordable to the average family. He wanted everyone to have the chance to live comfortably.

Mr. Bradshaw also made sure that all beaches on St. Kitts and Nevis would remain open to the public. I remember that, many years ago, a gentleman from the United States bought some land in Jones Estate on Nevis. He decided that he didn't want any local folks to walk on "his" beach. Mr. Bradshaw came over from St. Kitts and stopped the gentleman from building walls telling him that all beaches are open to the public.

Mr. Bradshaw, or "Papa" Bradshaw, as folks called him, in my opinion was truly a man of great faith in God and in his people regardless of their political affiliation. He loved all the people. He was more concerned about the poor than about wealth and fame.

In 1977, Mr. Bradshaw took ill and went off Island for treatment, returning thereafter to St. Kitts. What amazed me about Premier Bradshaw was that even when he was ill, he always stayed in touch with his people on St. Kitts and on Nevis. He was more concerned about his people's well-being than himself.

Mr. Bradshaw's condition worsened in January 1978, and he died in May of that same year after leading the country for more than 28 years. He was a great statesman, a man for all people. The airport on St. Kitts bears his name in memory of his contributions. To this day I remain thankful for his contributions--a job well done!

In 1970, Simeon Daniel and the late Ivor Stevens formed NRP, the Nevis Reformation Party, to fight the Federal Government, led by Premier Robert L. Bradshaw, with the goal of having either independence or self-government for Nevis. This was no easy task. Premier Bradshaw called for elections in 1971. Nevis held only two seats in the National Assembly at the time.

Mr. Stevens won, but Mr. Daniel, who was a young lawyer, lost to Fred Parris. Nevertheless, Mr. Daniel never gave up. He kept on fighting for Nevis to have self-rule. It was quite a battle. Mr. Bradshaw, who was a strong-willed fellow, said that "no way" he was going to let Nevis leave the State.

Nevis would have to remain under the St. Kitts Administration as long as Mr. Bradshaw was Premier of both St. Kitts and Nevis. When Mr. Bradshaw called for a snap election in December 1975, Mr. Daniel won a seat in the National Assembly defeating Fred Parris who had only served one term.

In 1976, Mr. Daniel and Mr. Stevens held a referendum on which ninety percent of the people of Nevis voted for either independence from St. Kitts or a return to direct rule under Great Britain. But Mr. Bradshaw did not recognize the vote. He said it was illegal thus stalling the process. Daniel and Stevens had no choice but to remain in the House of Assembly as opposition (or minority party) members.

When Premier Bradshaw died, his Vice-Premier, C.A. Paul Southwell, took over. However, during a trip to St. Lucia to meet with Caribbean heads of government, he took ill, and in May of 1979, he died having served only one year.

Upon Southwell's death, Lee Moore became Premier. Moore called for elections on February 18, 1980, in which the Labor Party won only four seats. Thus he either had to form a coalition government with the NRP or resign himself to becoming the opposition party.

Dr. Kennedy Simmons, leader of the opposition party, the People's Action Movement (PAM), came over to Nevis. PAM had won three seats and the NRP two.

The two parties formed the first coalition government in the history of St. Kitts and Nevis. Mr. Stevens of NRP became Minister of Public Works, Labor and Industry. Mr. Daniel became Minister of Finance and Minister of Nevis Affairs.

That was the start of the development in Nevis of an adequate water supply and more stable electrical power. In the 1970's, Nevis had suffered from a lot of load shedding. Everyone in Nevis only received four hours of electrical power daily. Charlestown was the exception--it had power most of the time.

Mr. Daniel, as Minister of Finance, ordered two new generating plants to provide a stable power source for his people. He also ordered the drilling of more water wells. Before they were operative, water in Nevis had been in short supply.

We, the people of Nevis, should keep alive the memory of these two great leaders who worked for the best interests of their constituents. Their actions are what started the development of Nevis. We, those who grew up in such hard times, should always thank Mr. Daniel and the late Mr. Stevens. They were true leaders who made life better for the next generation.

In 1982, Dr. Simmons talked about independence from Great Britain. Mr. Daniel and Mr. Stevens agreed to seek independence with the proviso that the proposed Constitution contains a clause stating that if 67 percent of the voters of Nevis vote in favor of separation from St. Kitts, then Nevis will be free from all control by the St. Kitts Administration.

Dr. Simmons agreed, and on September 19, 1983, St. Kitts and Nevis were declared an independent member of the British Commonwealth.

Nevis was allowed to have its own Premier, and Dr. Simmons became the first federal Prime Minister. Federal elections are held every five years, and local elections on Nevis are also held every five years.

So Mr. Daniel and Mr. Stevens made it possible for Nevis to have self-government. Mr. Daniel, the first Premier of Nevis, governed from 1980 to 1992. It was his Administration that brought the Four Seasons Resort to Nevis.

Construction began in 1989, and the resort opened its doors on Valentine's Day 1991. As the Island's second largest employer exceeded only by the Nevis Island Administration, we have much to thank Mr. Daniel for.

The coalition government held power for fifteen years during which Dr. Simmons made many improvements on St. Kitts as well. He started work on the deepwater port, attracted funds to build a highway the full length of the Southern Peninsula, and expanded the airport.

But in July of 1995, the Labor Party, led by Dr. Denzil Douglas, won a landslide victory winning the majority of the votes in every polling place. Dr. Douglas, who is from St. Paul, the same parish represented by Robert L. Bradshaw, has been re-elected with increasing margins of victory ever since, most recently in January of 2010.

. Douglas has worked consistently to transform St. Kitts from a sugar-based economy to one emphasizing the service sector.

The Port of Basseterre has been completely overhauled. Prime Minister Douglas has worked to eliminate poverty and to make home ownership and adequate health care available for all. Mr. Douglas has encouraged young people to become proprietors by operating gift shops, small farms, or crafts and woodworking businesses.

I have learned that Nevis has a rich history as well as a long involvement with the United States. Many American citizens love this island and own property here because of the friendliness of our people. Our motto is, "Country above self". The people of Nevis take care of our heritage by keeping our island clean and by protecting our coastline.

I have traveled a lot to many, many islands. Nevis is one of the cleanest you will find around the Caribbean. "Cleanliness is next to Godliness." We live by that rule.

So where am I now in 2011? I am 52 years old. I have fulfilled my lifelong dream, but I still keep dreaming. I have a guesthouse, a taxi service, and a fruit and vegetable garden in which I grow produce for sale. Since 2006, I have rented a couple of my units to the Cotton Ground Police Department since their old quarters in the village were inadequate.

I have traveled quite a bit including three trips to the United States and visits to several of the islands in the Eastern Caribbean. I am not afraid of the sea today, but I would not go on a cruise. I prefer to fly. I do take the ferry to St. Kitts however. I have no problem with that.

I have only casual contact with my family members who are still living. I never invite them to visit me in my home because I work hard all day, and when I get home, I just want to relax on the couch and maybe watch a little TV. I don't have the energy to entertain. My brother, Patrick, has returned to Nevis and is working at the Four Seasons Resort, but we just exchange brief greetings when we cross paths.

Although I was baptized a Catholic, and my mother was a Methodist, I attend the St. Thomas Anglican Church on a fairly regular basis. I am a firm believer in God, and I know that he is still watching over me. I believe that if we trust in God, He will protect us.

On June 1, 2010, I was driving from Vance W. Amory Airport toward Cotton Ground. I was traveling along the straight stretch below Round Hill at about 30 MPH. This is an area where there are always stray cattle both on the roadsides and often on the paved surface as they cross from one side to the other.

All of a sudden, a black bull ran out of the bush and crossed right in front of my SUV. I tried to brake, but the bull was too close, and I couldn't avoid hitting it. The impact damaged the front end of my taxi, which is only three years old, but at least I wasn't hurt.

If I had been driving fast, I would have been killed. I believe the good I have done is why I am still here. I have had so many close calls on this journey we call life that I know God has a reason for my still being here. I must work for Him all of my life as I am here for a purpose. My calling is not to serve myself but to serve others. "If any man will put himself to serve others, it will not be in vain." God will reward us with great blessings through his son, Jesus Christ.

It's not that I am perfect--none of us is, but if we can do some good for someone, in turn, God will reward us. The fact that a person like me who should have been killed so many times is still here has nothing to do with me. It is God's goodness and mercy that follows me because I try to help others.

I'm a pretty conservative guy. I can't remember ever doing any of the crazy stuff that other youngsters often do. I certainly never tried any dangerous daredevil stunts. I am a man of simple tastes. I still love to read. I suppose it is no surprise that I have found the Holy Bible to be the most influential book I have read.

I watch the Discovery Channel and other informative TV programs. I eat in restaurants on occasion, but I don't have a favorite place. The fact is that I love to cook and prefer to eat at home. I don't go to bars because I want to avoid trouble. Also, I was never much interested in dancing. I have a glass of wine at home every day, and, occasionally, I'll have a glass of Guinness. I'm not much into Caribbean music. I prefer gospel singing.

Well, I promised to tell you what I have learned. If you want to survive when things get you down, you have to have the willpower to endure. Never accept failure. Pick up the pieces and try again. The struggle will make you stronger.

Life is never easy. But God is good all the time. If you give a helping hand to someone today, tomorrow someone will do the same for you. Never give up. There is always a light at the end of the tunnel.

At times in our life we are called on to do some helpful act for someone. It may be an elderly person who needs our help. It may be hungry children who need to be fed. It may be a sick person who needs to be cared for. I have learned over the years that even in the 21st century, if you are good to someone, it will pay off--the goodness will come back to you.

Be good to the poor. You may need their help some day. As we say on Nevis, "Hand come, hand go, roast yam grow." If you do good in this life, in return the good will follow you. "Surely goodness and mercy will follow me all the days of my life and I shall dwell in the house of the Lord forever." (Psalm 23)

Plan for the future, but live for today. You never know when your end might come. Be willing to sacrifice to achieve your goals. Nothing comes easy. Be creative. Use your imagination to solve problems or open new doors.

The secret of living a long, healthy life is to eat homegrown vegetables, drink bush tea, make everything fresh from scratch, raise your own chickens, and get your exercise by working hard.

Judge people by their character. Pay no attention to color, religion, economic status. If they are not good people, pass them by. If they are good, show them love. Respect people always and greet them properly.

I believe that the harder you work the luckier you'll be. Money gained by illegal means doesn't last. There is a story of two women who had clothes to wash.

One of them washes the clothes, hangs them out to dry and gives thanks to God. The other waits for God to come and wash the clothes. Praying will help you a lot, but you have to work hard too. If you do, God will help.

Learn from your elders. Look for mentors, not gangsters. Young people need to learn to listen in order to get ahead.

So, Dear Reader, this is my message. If I can make it, anyone can. All of you can do better. You can make your dreams come true. I'm still dreaming and still working hard. I hope you will join me. Come, take my hand...

I wish you all peace, joy and love,

OZZIE

Made in the USA
Charleston, SC
25 October 2013